RICKY TIMS

DESERT VISIONS

RHAPSODY QUILTS

- **DESIGN COMPANION VOL. 4 TO *RICKY TIMS' RHAPSODY QUILTS***
- **FULL-SIZE FREEZER PAPER PATTERN ▪ BONUS APPLIQUÉ DESIGNS & IDEAS**

C&T PUBLISHING

Text copyright © 2009 by Ricky Tims

Artwork copyright © 2009 by C&T Publishing, Inc., and Ricky Tims

Publisher: Amy Marson

Creative Director: Gailen Runge

Editor: Liz Aneloski

Technical Editors: Ellen Pahl and Teresa Stroin

Copyeditor/Proofreader: Wordfirm Inc.

Cover/Book Designer: Kristen Yenche

Page Layout Artist: Kerry Graham

Production Coordinator: Zinnia Heinzmann

Illustrator: Aliza Shalit

Photography by Christina Carty-Francis and Diane Pedersen of C&T Publishing, Inc., unless otherwise noted

Published by C&T Publishing, Inc., P.O. Box 1456, Lafayette, CA 94549

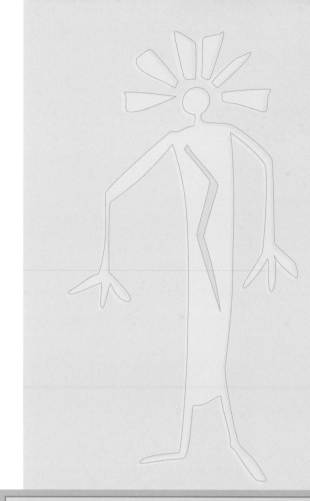

CONTENTS

INTRODUCTION

Many of you know I was born in Texas, and that I'm a misplaced Texan living in Colorado. I recently learned, however, that the old borders for the Republic of Texas (1846) extended way up into portions of what is now the state of Colorado. The tiny town I live in—La Veta—is actually located within those old Texas boundaries. That was a fun fact to learn!

While growing up in Texas, I naturally was influenced by the artistic themes of the Wild West. The images of coyotes, cacti, horseshoes, barbed wire, cattle skulls, cowboy hats, and boots have been a part of my daily life since I was born. In Colorado, I am surrounded by contemporary Native American artistry and by the designs of the ancient Fremont and Anasazi petroglyphs and pictographs of the Southwest.

The art and imagery associated with the Western United States has always been popular, and the artistic lines between the West and the Southwest, both contemporary and ancient, are hazy. Therefore, it seemed natural for me to blend these themes in a book of Western/Southwestern Rhapsody designs that might inspire you to create a quilt to accent an area of your home suited for these themes. You may also appreciate the fact that these designs tend to be appropriate for quilts made for husbands, fathers, and sons.

Each *Rhapsody Quilts Design Companion* is created with the assumption that you will utilize my book *Ricky Tims' Rhapsody Quilts* as the primary how-to source. By combining the basic information from the original book with the specific instructions here, you can re-create my *Raven and the Wind* Rhapsody quilt (full-size pattern included on the pullout), or you can use one of the alternate skeletons (pages 8–9) and adapt any of the thematic appliqué designs (on the pullout) to fit your skeleton to create your own Western/Southwestern-style Rhapsody quilt.

In creating the appliqué motifs, I have not tried to replicate any designs from actual Native American art, nor have I traced or copied any ancient designs. Instead, I have created original designs that capture the essence or spirit of the imagery I have experienced in the West and Southwest. You are welcome to use my designs for your Rhapsody quilt. If you intend to replicate contemporary designs from other sources, remember always to get written permission from the artist or designer before doing so.

As always, I welcome photos of your completed projects. Contact me via *www.rickytims.com*.

Quilt On!

Raven and the Wind

Raven and the Wind, 60¹/₂″ × 60¹/₂″, completed in 2008. Designed, pieced, machine appliquéd, and machine quilted by Ricky Tims.

Materials

Fabric amounts are based on 42˝-wide fabric.

Refer to Selecting Fabrics (page 35) for guidance as needed.

Fabric A: 2¾ yards

Fabric B: 3⅝ yards

Fabric C: 1¾ yards

Fabric D: 1¼ yards

Fabric E: ⅞ yard

Assorted fabrics in coordinating colors for appliqués: ⅔ yard total

Binding: ⅝ yard

Backing: 3⅞ yards

Batting: 66˝ × 66˝

18˝-wide fusible web: 8 yards

Thread: assorted colors to contrast with appliqué fabrics

Cutting and Preparing the Fabrics

For these steps, refer to Preparing the Master Template (page 34) and Preparing the Units (pages 38–39) for guidance as needed.

1. Use the pattern on the pullout at the back of the book to create full-size templates for the quilt background. You will need to trace the center templates (pieces 1 and 2) to make 4 pieces of each. Then tape them together to create the complete templates for pieces 1 and 2. Be sure to transfer all registration marks.

2. Iron the freezer paper templates to the right side of the following fabrics and rough cut the fabric about ½˝ from the edge of the freezer paper.

From Fabric A, cut 1 of piece 1, and 4 *each* of pieces 3, 3 reverse, and 7.

From Fabric B, cut 1 of piece 2, and 4 *each* of pieces 6, 6 reverse, and 8.

From Fabric C, cut 4 *each* of pieces 4 and 5.

3. Stay stitch around each template and add the registration marks in the seam allowances.

4. Trim the seam allowances to a scant ¼˝, remove the freezer paper, and place the fabric pieces on a design wall.

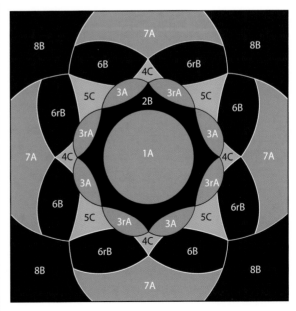

Skeleton layout—Numbers indicate piece numbers, and letters indicate fabric.

Adding the Appliqués

For these steps, refer to Machine Appliqué Techniques—Fear Not the "A" Word (pages 47–57) as needed. After cutting background pieces 1–8, use the remainder of the fabrics and the assorted fabrics in coordinating colors for the appliqués.

1. Trace the appliqué designs from the pullout onto the paper side of the fusible web.

2. Adhere the fusible web to the fabrics listed below, or to your chosen fabrics, and prepare the appliqués.

Fabric A: bird body in piece 6 and designs in pieces 4, 5, and 8

Fabric B: raven in piece 1

Fabric C: wider designs in piece 2 and wings in pieces 6 and 6 reverse

Fabric D: tall, treelike designs in piece 2; Kokopelli in pieces 3 and 3 reverse; beak and thunderbolt in pieces 6 and 6 reverse; and inner corner appliqués in piece 8

Fabric E: detail designs in pieces 3 and 3 reverse and appliqués in piece 7

Assorted fabrics: remaining designs in piece 1 and bird head in pieces 6 and 6 reverse

3. Refer to the diagram and to the photo on page 4 of this book to fuse the appliqués onto the appropriate background pieces.

4. Stitch around the edges of each appliqué shape, using a machine single or double blanket stitch and threads that contrast in color to the various appliqué fabrics.

Assembling the Quilt

For these steps, refer to No-Pins Precision Curved Piecing (pages 38–41), Sewing the Pieces Together (pages 57–58), Preparing Units for Set-In Curved Corners (pages 62–63), Setting in a Curved Corner (pages 64–65), Preparing Units for Set-In Circles (page 66), and Sewing the Circle in the Hole (pages 67–68) for guidance as needed.

Refer to the skeleton layout diagram on page 5 of this book. Beginning with the center (piece 1), assemble the skeleton by adding pieces in numerical order, aligning the stay-stitching and registration marks and straightening the curves as you sew.

Finishing the Quilt

For these steps, refer to Tips for Quilting Your Rhapsody Quilt (page 69) for guidance as needed.

1. Mark, layer, and baste your quilt in preparation for quilting.

2. Machine quilt as desired.

3. Trim the batting and backing even with the raw edge of the quilt top.

4. Cut 7 strips $2\frac{1}{8}'' \times 42''$ from the binding fabric. Use diagonal seams to sew the strips together end to end and use them to bind the edges of the quilt.

Skeleton with appliqués in place

ADDITIONAL DESIGNS TO TRY

Ten New Skeletons

Here are ten additional skeleton designs you can choose from to create your own Desert Visions—or any other—Rhapsody quilt. Simply enlarge the pattern of your choice to the desired size, as described in Creating a Full-Size Pattern (pages 30–33), and add appliqué. On the pullout pages of this book, you'll find a variety of appliqué designs, inspired by the American West and by Native American and ancient Native American themes, that you can use as is or adapt for use with any of these skeletons.

Skeleton 3

Skeleton 4

Skeleton 1

Skeleton 5

Skeleton 2

Skeleton 9

Skeleton 6

Skeleton 10

Skeleton 7

Skeleton 8—Page 14 shows this skeleton transformed into fabric with appliqué added.

Western and Native American Appliqué Designs

The patterns on the pullout page provide a wide variety of appliqué designs inspired by the American West and by Native American and ancient Native American themes. You can use many of these designs as is to fit the skeletons on pages 8–9. In most cases, however, you will need to reduce, enlarge, or customize them to fit your particular space. Reshape the appliqué designs to fit the space; don't reshape the spaces to fit the appliqué.

 *If you like, adapt some of the appliqué patterns—including those on the pattern for Raven and the Wind—to create designs for quilting.*

The following illustrations show how to adapt the designs to fit your space by reshaping the appliqués and adding filler designs.

Altered design with filler accent shapes

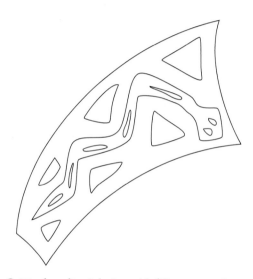

Original appliqué design with filler accent shapes

Original appliqué design with filler accent shapes

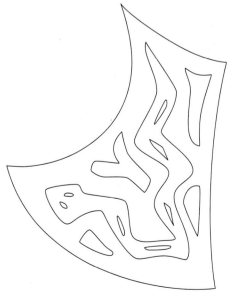

Altered design with filler accent shapes

QUILTS FOR INSPIRATION

Dance by Marian Pierce, 82″ × 84″

"When Ricky presented me with the challenge of designing a Rhapsody quilt depicting aspects of my Colorado lifestyle, little did I realize the journey that lay ahead. During hours of machine embroidery, appliqué, and quilting, I revisited memories of childhood and all things cowboy that have shaped my life today. The process took me through many twists and turns, what Ricky calls rafting on a rushing river, and I have loved every minute of the ride."

Rhapsody for the White Buffalo Calf Woman by Jan Potter, 60″ x 60″

"I drew the rhapsody design at Ricky's seminar in Mesa, Arizona, but at that time had never made a quilt and really had no interest in making one. I attended the seminar with some friends in a sewing group I had just joined, and I thought I would use some of the techniques to make wearable art! I took the design home and put it away. Then when I attended a retreat with Ricky in 2007, I came armed with this design. By this time, I had only been quilting for two years and still had so much to learn. But I just kept plodding along in my slow methodical way, following each of the steps Ricky outlines in his book. The joy of completing a project like this one has really boosted my self-esteem. Now the only thing that holds me back is not having enough time to make quilts from all of the ideas in my head."

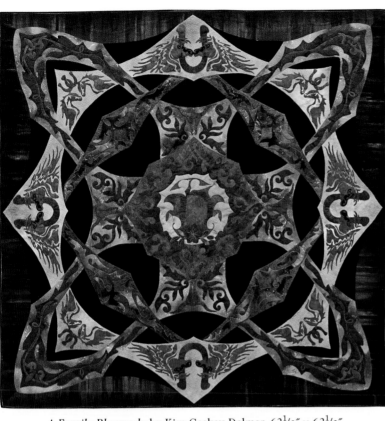

"Inspired by the works of Ricky Tims, this Rhapsody quilt combines precise techniques of machine appliqué, curved piecing, and extensive machine quilting. The challenge of designing the skeletal pattern was only the first step! Flowing curves are mirrored and reversed. Like a rhapsody in music, this piece allowed creative expression of theme and design."

A Family Rhapsody by Kim Caskey-Dalmer, 63$\frac{1}{2}$˝ × 63$\frac{1}{2}$˝

"When Ricky announced the theme of his next book, this quilt magically appeared in my head! I wanted the background to reflect the Southwest, so I designed the skeleton to include hoodoos, buttes, and arches in southwest colors. The petroglyphs are adapted from photos of actual petroglyphs; reworking them to fit the space was a fun challenge. The trapunto echoes the graphic nature of the petroglyphs. I already have two more Rhapsody quilts in my head ready to go!"

Ancient Rhapsodies by Cindy Neville, 51˝ × 51˝

Skeleton 8 (page 9 of this book) without appliqué

Note that the arcs would be paper pieced to create the sharp, narrow spikes of black and tan.

Skeleton 8 with appliqué

Skeleton without appliqué

Skeleton with appliqué

ABOUT RICKY

Ricky Tims has successfully blended two diverse passions into one very unique and interesting career. His skills as a pianist, composer, and producer have been affirmed by the thousands who have heard his music. His success as a quilter is equally significant.

He is known in the international world of quilting as an enthusiastic and encouraging teacher, an award-winning quilter, and a talented and spellbinding speaker. His innovative and entertaining presentations feature live music and humor, combined with scholarly insights and wisdom. His quilts have been displayed worldwide and are highly regarded as excellent examples of contemporary quilts with traditional appeal. He is currently the cohost of *The Quilt Show*, an Internet-based show for quilters that also features Alex Anderson, C&T author and former host of HGTV's *Simply Quilts*.

Ricky began designing and making quilts in 1991. In 2002, he was selected as one of the Thirty Most Distinguished Quilters in the World. He maintains an international schedule of teaching and speaking engagements, presents *Ricky Tims' Super Quilt Seminars* in select cities throughout the United States, and holds weeklong retreats in La Veta, a tiny mountain town located in south-central Colorado. He and life partner, Justin Shults, own Tims Art Quilt Studio and Gallery, a space dedicated to promoting quilting as art.

Ricky is passionate about quilting and is delighted to share his experience and enthusiasm with quilters of every level of expertise. He is the author of five previous books with C&T Publishing: *Ricky Tims' Convergence Quilts* (2003), *Ricky Tims' Rhapsody Quilts* (2007), *Feathers & Urns—Rhapsody Quilts*

(2008), *Baskets & Flowers—Rhapsody Quilts* (2008), and *Celtic Fantasy—Rhapsody Quilts* (2008). He is challenged by creativity in all forms and encourages individuals to cultivate self-expression, reach for the unreachable, and believe in the impossible.

Quilting is a relatively new interest compared with Ricky's lifelong passion for music. He began formal music lessons at the age of three. He is a pianist, conductor, composer, arranger, music producer, and performing artist. Tims' music is neither classical, new age, pop, nor world, and yet it could fall under any of those classifications.

Sacred Age, Ricky's most recent recording, was released in January 2006. The album project, featuring solo piano infused with Native American instruments, string orchestra, and vocal orchestrations, was created to suggest the beauty, majesty, and spirit of the Spanish Peaks region of southern Colorado. Tims' music has wide appeal for a diverse audience and has been described as "George Winston meets Carlos Nakai meets Yanni."

Visit Ricky's website: www.rickytims.com.

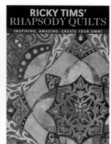

For a list of other fine books from C&T Publishing, ask for a free catalog:

C&T Publishing, Inc.
P.O. Box 1456
Lafayette, CA 94549

(800) 284-1114
Email: ctinfo@ctpub.com
Website: www.ctpub.com

C&T Publishing's professional photography services are now available to the public. Visit us at www.ctmediaservices.com.